10 Strategies for LOW cost Listing Leads

By

Jason Morris

Join the Facebook group Real Estate Agents that REALLY work

Go to www.JasonMorrisPrelistingpackage.com and get my free script book1

Table of Contents

Introduction
Tools you will need
FSBOs
FRBOs
Expired Listings
Sphere of Influence
Open houses
Geographical farming
CourtHouse filings
Tax liens
Foreclosure Auctions/lists
Leads you can find everyday
Bonus 1: The $100,000 notebook plan
Bonus #2 Building a Massive followup Plan
Bonus #3 - 10 follow up call, email and text scripts to use for your seller leads

Go to www.JasonMorrisPrelistingpackage.com and get my free script book2

Introduction

One of the biggest things I see in the real estate industry is that agents no longer are trained to supply their own leads. New and old agents get stuck in the trap of buying leads from sources like Zillow or Realtor (dot) com.

I am thankful that I was taught very early that the best way to find real estate deals and listings is to find people with problems and learn how to help them solve those problems.

Now I am not saying buying leads or data does not work. There are plenty of agents out there buying leads and making significant returns on their marketing dollars spent.

However, there are a lot of leads out there that NO ONE is focusing on and if you are willing to do a little extra work and be a little creative you can unlock some lead sources that have very little to no competition.

I have been in the real estate sales business for 20 years. I started the Facebook group Real estate agents that REALLY work. I have trained thousands of agents

Go to www.JasonMorrisPrelistingpackage.com and get my free script book3

over the last 7 years on ways to effectively build listing heavy businesses.

The goal of this book is to give you some ideas and some lead sources and strategies that are often overlooked by most agents in the industry. Most of these lead sources are no cost or low cost.

Go to www.JasonMorrisPrelistingpackage.com and get my free script book4

Tools you will need

1. Redx GeoLeads - I recommend using this subscription service for several different reasons. The biggest is because you can often find peoples phone numbers and email addresses using it. It is also extremely versatile and can be used in so many different ways for lead generation

    Once you get phone numbers and email addresses you can upload them to Facebook and run ad campaigns against them, as well as, direct mail, make calls, add to drip campaigns and have a whole integrated marketing plan.

2. CRM - A very user friendly CRM is like gold. Actually it is your goldmine. You just have to fill it up and

3. A notebook that stays in your car

4. Go to www.JasonMorrisPrelistingpackage.com and get my free script book along with other tools and training to get more listings.

FSBOs

For Sale by Owners
A lot of agents overlook these or just do not like calling them. Really though, how can you get a better lead source? These people are going out and pretty much raising their hand and trying to sell their own house.

The reason I mention these leads first is because I think it is a lead source that should be part of every agents plan. I even wrote a book "How to be a FSBO Master" that you can find on Amazon that gives you a complete system on how to work these leads, follow up with them and what to do at the listing appointment.

Here are a few places you should spend a few minutes looking everyday for these leads

Craigslist - A lot of agents skip this website, but if you sort through the agent listings there are new properties posted all the time. I would suggest printing them out as you find them and keeping a folder of them. As you make contact, add them to your CRM

Go to www.JasonMorrisPrelistingpackage.com and get my free script book6

ZIllow - The biggest website of them all. You don't have to pay to go on and look at the FSBOs in your area.

Facebook MarketPlace - This is a great FSBO lead source. The issue most agents have is they try to list the property through private messages. The purpose of your message should be to get the person on the phone and then on the phone call attempt to set an appointment.

<u>A simple script is:</u>

        Agent: What is a good phone number for you?
        Seller: (gives you their phone number)
        Agent: What is the best time to give you a call?
        Seller: (let them answer)

Then you call them at that time.

It is really that easy. Use this same script with craigslist ads for FSBOs that do not have phone numbers

Facebook Buy/sell groups - I do not know why but often when homes are posted in these groups they often do not show up in the MarketPlace section on facebook. It would not be a bad idea to scroll through these for 10 to 15 minutes a day looking for properties that people have posted.

Go to www.JasonMorrisPrelistingpackage.com and get my free script book7

FSBO signs - With the real estate market slowing down I feel like I am seeing more and more of those red and white FSBO signs popping up all over the place.

I would recommend that you make it a practice to never drive by another one of these signs without stopping, writing down the phone number, address and even snapping a picture of the house and sign.

One thing I have done over the years that has been very effective is to just go ahead and call them quickly while you are sitting in the driveway.

I know we are all busy but adding an additional 10 to 15 minutes to your commute times just doing your regular routine and driving through a couple of neighborhoods or taking a different way home can pay off big over time.

Go to www.JasonMorrisPrelistingpackage.com and get my free script book8

FRBOs

For rent by owners

I have had this idea for years that most people never set out to be landlords on purpose. Most people that are landlords only have 1 or 2 properties. Usually they inherited a property or had a property they couldn't sell, so they rented it out.

On top of that, there are a lot of really tired landlords out there. If they do manage to get that perfect tenants that stays for years, good for them. The reality is though, on a long enough time frame, every tenant moves or is evicted.

Typically it is rare that a tenant moves out after a year of living in a place and the property doesn't have any wear and tear or is improved in any way. Typically carpet and paint is a minimum plus removing furniture, trash and who knows what else.

There are a few things that we know about these leads also.

1. Most leases are only for 12 months or less
2. No one knows when even the best tenant will have a difficult time and have to move out or

Go to www.JasonMorrisPrelistingpackage.com and get my free script book

just can pay. Especially in a changing economy.
3. A property can be sold with a tenant in place
4. If the owner has a mortgage, it is due every month even if the tenant don't pay

A good strategy for this lead type is to use your CRM and database these property owners. If you added just an average of 5 FRBOs to your database a week, you would add 250 leads a year to your database. That is 250 property owners that are going to have a lease ending or a tenant moving in the next 12 months.

Your job is to stay in contact with these owners until something happens. I would recommend an integrated approach to staying in contact with these owners. Here are a few ideas on ways to stay in contact after that first initial conversation.

1. A regular phone call about properties going on and off the market in the neighborhood their property is in.
2. A text to your database
3. A regular email - this could even be them being set up on a MLS alert for properties coming available in their neighborhood along with a follow up call or voice mail
4. A voicemail drop to your database
5. A targeted Facebook ad, specifically targeting landlords
6. A quarterly mailer

Go to www.JasonMorrisPrelistingpackage.com and get my free script book10

With this lead type, follow up is the key. You need to catch them when they have a vacancy or a bad tenant.

Go to www.JasonMorrisPrelistingpackage.com and get my free script book11

Expired Listings

I would like to assume that you are a real estate agent and already know what an expired listing is, but for those of you that do not:

An expired listing is when a listing agreement ends with an agent and it shows up on your MLS as being "expired" or is just no longer on the market.

I know many of you reading this have tried to re-list expired listings before. A lot of agents give up or think there are too many people calling them.

The easiest way to get phone numbers, email addresses and an address where the tax bill goes to (or owner lives) is to subscribe to a data service like REDx. You can use the link www.JasonMorrisREDx.com and they waive the set up fee for you.

I want to cover a couple of other options you have to try to list them, other than just making calls.

1. **Door knocking expireds**

    If you choose to go knock on the door of an expired listing you need to make sure you

Go to www.JasonMorrisPrelistingpackage.com and get my free script book12

are set up for success.

a. Have a flier or some sort of information that you can leave in the door. What you want is a call to action, not a marketing piece where you are trying to list it but one that they respond to and contact or call you.

I always recommend you keep it very simple. A handwritten note that says "do you still want to sell your house? Call me (phone number)" works very well.

b. If they are home, I would recommend the conversation starting with "do you want to sell your home?" If they say yes, continue the conversation by getting their phone number and email, then setting up a time to actually come back and list it. A stranger showing up at someone's house asking to come in is typically not going to be a welcoming visit.

c. Follow up is the key to getting listings with any lead type. A "no" is not typically rejecting you, it is them rejecting the idea that you are presenting to them in the moment.

2. **Phone calls**

I still feel like, even in 2024, the best practice is to get someone on the phone. The problem a lot of agents have is they miss the purpose of the phone call. The call is not to list the property, the purpose is to set an appointment to list the property.

Here are a few tips to help you when making these calls.

1. Always use a script. If you ask the same questions over and over, it does not take long until you know all the answers to the questions you are asking. Once you talk to 50 sellers, 100 sellers, 1000 sellers, you will almost be able to anticipate the response they are going to give you before they even give it to you.

2. Eliminate the word "listing from your vocabulary when talking to a seller. Instead of talking about "listing" their house, you should talk about "selling" their house. Remember they just

Go to www.JasonMorrisPrelistingpackage.com and get my free script book

"listed" with another agent, it didn't work out. That is why it expired.

3. Watch your tonality when talking to a seller. If you are not confident about your plan and what you are saying. They won't be confident about your plan and you either.

4. Follow up is the key! I would be willing to bet just a small fraction of 1% of expired calls end in them saying "yes, bring the paperwork right now and let me sign it". It may take 10 to 12 conversations or more before you set an appointment and actually list their property. This goes for all types of leads.

5. Have a plan. Most agents are constantly just shooting from the hip and hoping things work out. You need a full sales process and plan to be able to consistently take listings. I wrote a book called "How to be an Expired Master" that is available on Amazon. In that book I go through an entire process to help you take more expired listings.

3. **Texting Expires**

Go to www.JasonMorrisPrelistingpackage.com and get my free script book15

It is a busy world we live in. Most of us are used to just texting people rather than picking up the phone. The problem most agents have is they try to skip right to the point and send a huge text thinking that somehow this seller will be super impressed and just call them to relist the house ASAP.

But just like when one of your friends sends you a HUGE text, the chances of you reading it before you get distracted by the next thing is very small. Here are some text scripts that you can use for the initial contact

1. "Do you still want to sell the house at (address)?"
2. "Can you call me at your earliest convenience about the house at (address)?"
3. "Are you the owner of (address)?"

These texts are very simple with a "yes" or "no" response. If they respond with a "yes" your next text should always be

"When is a good time to call you?"

Set up a time to call and call at that time.

4. **Facebook ads**

Go to www.JasonMorrisPrelistingpackage.com and get my free script book

If you subscribe to a service like REDx you can take the phone numbers/emails and upload them to Facebook to create a custom audience. For just a few dollars a day you can have an ad running and showing up in their newsfeed on Facebook.

5. **Direct Mail**

The reason I included this as a way to get more listings for expireds is because there just are not many people sending mail anymore.

Go to www.JasonMorrisPrelistingpackage.com and get my free script book17

Sphere of Influence

I know, I know… Some of you reading this right now are going "I know about this already" but the problem is most agents do not know how to nurture a sphere of influence at all.

I'm going to give you a quick strategy to get the most out of your sphere of influence.

1. Go through your phone and your facebook account. Make a list of every person you actually know. The ones you have met in person.

2. Now go thru that list you made and we are going to make a 2nd list of people. These people are the ones that you have actually sent you business in the past and ones that are what I am going to refer to as "Power Connectors"

    1. **Power connector** - This is a person that regularly comes in contact with a lot of

Go to www.JasonMorrisPrelistingpackage.com and get my free script book18

people. Typically this person is a trusted figure in the community or area.

Here are a few examples:
(of course there are more than this)

- Pastors of a local church
Small convenience store owners
- Civic group organizers
- Hardware store employees or managers
- Local Handyman

These are just a few examples. Of Course there are a lot more. Be creative and think about who you know and who they know.

Ill give you a few examples from my career.

Convenience store owners

Go to www.JasonMorrisPrelistingpackage.com and get my free script book

I met a couple that owned a small convenience store. This store didn't sell gas but it served breakfast and lunch. The occasionally served dinner. The couple actually worked in the store and the husband was the cook. They were genuinely very nice people.

I sold a property for them and as a common practice of mine, I looked them up to see what other properties they own in the county. Turned out they had a large tract of land and another house that was a rental. I ended up doing a couple of transactions with them on properties they personally owned.

The crazy thing was, they knew EVERYBODY in the area. They would hand out more of my business cards in a day sometimes than I could in a month! Every Time I was in the area, I made sure I stopped by. We shared pictures of our kids, life stories and I built a personal relationship with these people. For years these people sent me at least 2 to 3 transactions a year.

Political Consultant

For years, I was very involved in local politics. I think all agents should be to a certain extent. It is a great way to get exposure and oftentimes there are only 1 or 2 candidates running for a local office. It is a great way to meet influential people in your area.

This one political consultant in my area helped a lot of candidates and had been doing it for years! He knew

Go to www.JasonMorrisPrelistingpackage.com and get my free script book20

everybody that was anybody! We often had and have the same political views also.

After I got to know him, I would volunteer and give money to whoever his candidate was that he was helping. He knew that if he called me, it didn't matter if it was giving my time to make calls for a couple of hours, door knocking a neighborhood or just giving $100…. I was there and he could depend on me.

Over the course of our relationship, he continuously sent me people that needed help buying or selling a house. He was and has been one of the top people that would send me business in my area.

The Home owner Association (Hoa) Manager

I met a guy years ago that worked for an HOA management company. This was back when the market was in a downturn and the economy was not very good. We actually met because of a bad tenant that was in a property that I was managing.

The story was, this tenant of mine kept going out to the community swimming pool late at night and using it as his personal bathroom. I'm sure the call the Hoa manager made to me was equally as awkward and embarrassing as me getting the call and then having to call the tenant about it.

Go to www.JasonMorrisPrelistingpackage.com and get my free script book21

The thing about it was, as bad as it was, we had a sense of humor about it and bonded over the bad situation. I ended up evicting the tenant and building a relationship with the HOA manager.

During this time, short sales were almost normal. Over the next few years, everytime the HOA board met about delinquent HOA fees. He would bring up my name as someone that could help these people behind on HOA fees and behind on their mortgages.

The advantage was, if the owner sold through a short sale, the HOA would get something out of the sale of the property. If the bank foreclosed on the property, chances are the HOA would not get anything at all.

So every month or so, he would pass out my number to a handful of struggling homeowners in several communities and give me a glowing recommendation as someone that could help them.

The Mobile Home Park Manager

Homes and mobile homes on leased land in my area is a pretty common property type. The great thing also is, it is a niche that not many agents want to specialize in.

They managed about 500 home spots in this one community. Through several transactions and a lot of phone calls and questions, I got to know the people in the office. One thing I constantly made sure of is any

Go to www.JasonMorrisPrelistingpackage.com and get my free script book

back lot rent that was owed would get reported and paid as part of the sale.

I would regularly stop in, say hey and typically bring something with me. A dozen donuts, coffee, candy or just something random.

The main office sent me a deal a month for years.

Go to www.JasonMorrisPrelistingpackage.com and get my free script book

Open houses

In my coaching and training, I have often talked about not doing open houses. That has been my preference over the years. For me personally it is a time consuming process to do an open house correctly.

Most agents just stick out a sign about 10 minutes before an open house and then they just hope for the best.

The best way to have a "Productive" open house is to have a system.

Im going to give you a step by step list of what to do to make your open house as productive as possible.

1. Put out your signed the day before. Have signs and balloons going all the way out to a main road or highway.

   Put a sign in front of the house with the hours of the open house also.

2. Go door knock the entire neighborhood the day before. Make sure you have a basic flier or some marketing material that you can stick

Go to www.JasonMorrisPrelistingpackage.com and get my free script book

in doors and hand out that promotes the open house.

3. Show up about 30 minutes early. Make sure you have a sign in sheet and ask every person that walks in the door to sign in

4. The day after the open house, door knock the same neighborhood.

   Your door knocking script should to something like this

   "Hey Mr/Mrs neighbor, we has a great open house yesterday at (address) we had (x number of people) come through it I was wondering if you knew anyone else looking to sell in your neighborhood?"

Bonus
If you subscribe to Redx Geoleads, you can make calls to the neighborhood beforehand also. You can also do voice mail drops and run targeted Facebook ads for your open house to the list you get from GeoLeads.

Go to www.JasonMorrisPrelistingpackage.com and get my free script book

Geographical farming

A lot of agents forget or just don't know that this use to be the big lead generator in the real estate industry. It still works, you just have to have a plan to make it work.

Of course you can pick an area with about 1,000 homes in it and door knock them all. All it costs is your time and some print cost for marketing material. Do this monthly, leaving stuff on property owners doors and it wont take but a few months and people will start recognizing your name.

However if you combine that with a full integrated plan you can quickly become a celebrity in that local area.

- Here are some ideas.

  Door knock the whole area once a month leaving a marketing piece behind or just a simple black and white flier.

- Hold open houses for your listings and your offices listing at every home you can in your farming area.

- Pre-view every home that comes on the market in that area. Then use a 5-5-10 door

Go to www.JasonMorrisPrelistingpackage.com and get my free script book26

knock strategy on every home that you preview. This is where you door knock 5 homes to the right of the listing, 5 homes to the left of the listing and then 10 homes across the street. Then of course leave a marketing piece behind.

Subscribe to Geoleads by redx (www.JasonMorrisRedx.com)

- Call once a quarter every home in your geographic farm area. Try to have as many meaningful conversations as you can.

- Do voicemail drops for every listing that comes on the market in that area. Just something simple "Hey I wanted to let you know a new listing just came on the market at (address) it is priced at (price). I wanted to see if you knew anyone interested.

- Use the email address and start a newsletter or just listed/pending/solds in the area or even neighborhood.

- Use the date and run targeted ad on Social media.

Go to www.JasonMorrisPrelistingpackage.com and get my free script book

CourtHouse filings

I have always had this belief that if we can solve problems for people then we can take that ability to solve a problem and find a lot of clients all with the same problem.

One place I have learned you can find a lot of people with problems is at the courthouse. I am going to give you a list of things you can find digging in the public records and learning how to use public records to find clients.

Typically the people working at the courthouse are pretty nice and easy to work with. If you have questions, they will help put you in the right direction.

I am in South Carolina. So all of my experience is in the state I actually work in but you can take this information and these ideas and go down to the court house and find more leads than you can ever work.

I am going to give you the ideas. The systems to actually work these leads are up to you. I could probably write a book on each one of these things.

Go to www.JasonMorrisPrelistingpackage.com and get my free script book

Remember if you have geoleads and some creativity you can get in touch with a lot of these people or at least get in front of them.

Here are some ideas on how to get in touch with the leads you find at the courthouse.

1. Geoleads - look up numbers and email addresses to call and email
2. Facebook ads - use the data from geoleads to create a custom list.
3. Door knock
4. Door knock the neighbors house and ask how to get in touch with them
5. Direct mail
6. Social Media - look them up and message them
7. Text

Getting the leads and then getting in touch with the people can often be a little bit time consuming. If you don't have the money to hire a title company and buy the court house data, it is typically free for you to just go look it up yourself. Some counties are more advanced and you can even find it all online.

1. **Eviction Filings**

    What you are looking for is tired landlords. I believe that most people are not professional landlords. They typically only have 1 or 2

Go to www.JasonMorrisPrelistingpackage.com and get my free script book

properties. They decided to rent the property out either because it didn't sell or they had a mortgage and couldn't afford the mortgage on a house sitting empty.

I will tell you guys, as I am writing this book, I have a place right now that I have rented out for years. I've screened tenants, qualified them etc. I own 4 more in the same neighborhood, they all have been full since I bought them with the original tenants in them. For some reason, I can't seem to get a tenant in this one that stays. I am tired of renovating it and having to re-fill it. I am evicting someone right now. If a buyer or an agent contacted me today… They could buy it and I would probably give them a deal on it.

With the economy slowing down, the rent a lot of these landlords were getting a year ago, probably isn't the rent that they can get today. Most of the time, when a tenant moves out the place always needs paint and carpet.

2. **Code enforcement violations**

You wouldn't believe how many people build decks, garages, additions etc on a home and never pull a permit. Some of these people will never get caught and everything was built to code and is safe. They just didn't go through the proper permitting and inspections.

Depending on the city, county and state, the penalty could be anything from a small fine to them having to tear the addition down.

The problem most people have is they spent money to build a nice deck, they don't have the money or knowledge to correct the problem with the local government.

I have seen code enforcement get involved in issues where the owner has an excessive amount of trash on the property. Which seems like an easy issue and it is if there were just a few bags or trash. But when it really piles up, it could cost thousands in just dumpster fees and labor to get it removed.

Eventually if the problem isn't corrected, code enforcement has the authority to condemn a property.

3. **Condemned properties**

   A lot of agents and people thing once a property has been condemned that its over with. The property has to be torn down. That is often not the case. If the issue goes on long enough and the property starts to deteriorate then there is a chance that the property could get torn down and it ends up being at the expense of the property owner.

The thing to remember is, these properties are not benefiting the owner at all if they don't have the knowledge or financial capabilities to get the issue resolved. There are deals when looking at condemned properties.

A few years ago, I bought a property that was condemned. I talked to the seller. He told me that it was going to have to be torn down. Before making a deal with the seller, I went to the local county office, talked to code enforcement. All they wanted was the grass cut and broken windows replaced. Homeless people had been sleeping in it.

Another time, I helped a client buy a triplex that was condemned by the city. It was right downtown and a great location for a rental. He ended up paying $15,000 for it. It needed about $75,000 to fix all of the problems and get it back livable. That property today grosses about $3500 a month and would easily sell for about $400,000. At the time, in livable condition it was worth an easy $200,000.

Go to www.JasonMorrisPrelistingpackage.com and get my free script book

I will tell you 1 more story about working with condemned properties. I deal a lot with mobile homes. I got 2 mobile homes for free from a property owner a few years back. The owner didn't properly pull permits to set them up on the same property as his primary residence. He thought he could just add 2 more units, because he felt like he had room and it was his property. He ended up giving me the 2 mobile homes just to move them off of his property. If he didn't, they were going to condemn the property and turn off the electric to his home he was living in.

4. Homeowner association (HOA) liens

A lot of owners do not realize that you can own a property free and clear but if you do not pay the homeowner association fees, then they can foreclose on your property.

I see this often in my market. Especially several years ago when we were in a recession. People would pay their mortgage and just not pay their HOA fees.

Once that lien is filed, the clock is ticking for the foreclosure process to start. I have been to auctions and saw owners lose properties worth $100,000 over small amounts like

$5,000 in back HOA fees.

5. Homeowner Association (HOA) litigation

   Sometimes when the homeowners don't agree with the HOA or the developer, it results in litigation. This sort of chaos in a community has been a goldmine for me in the past. Once litigation is filed, a lot of agents do not understand what happens, so they just stay away from these properties thinking they won't be able to sell them.

   The reality is most litigation doesn't affect the entire community or condo development. With condos, it typically makes financing them a little more difficult. Learning the litigation process, reading the actual filing and networking with lenders that can finance condos in litigation are key to being able to help these homeowners get rid of what is a problem for them.

6. Pre-foreclosures

   Once a bank or lien holder files for foreclosure, it takes a little while. In some cases it can take a year or more to go through the court process.

   During that time the homeowner still has the

right to cure the problem and can sell it up until the time it is actually foreclosed on.

7. Probate

Every courthouse has a probate office. Typically you can get all of the information off of a probate filing for the executor of the estate and often, even the assets included in probate.

This does take a little work, but you can get a lot of information off of the filings.

8. Building permits

   It doesn't matter what market you are in, building permits are being filed everyday. I would look for the ones being filed by small local builders or by homeowners themselves. They may have another property they are going to be selling or it could be a home being built just to sell.

9. Permits for renovations

   There is a whole range of things people could be filing permits for. It could be something like a new roof on the house they live in. The thing you are looking for is investors that are filing permits to rehab a property.

Go to www.JasonMorrisPrelistingpackage.com and get my free script book

10. Applications to subdivide or develop property

Typically, it is my experience if you see someone filing an application for a minor subdivision, it isn't to just cut a lot off of a bigger tract for a family member. It is usually to subdivide a larger parcel into home lots to sell them. This is a great way to find small investors.

I met a guy about 15 years ago that specialized in what is typically called "Minor subdivisions". In my area this is 10 lots or less. It is an easy process. That requires not a whole lot more than an application and a survey. This guy bought tracts of land and put together land home packages with double wide mobile homes on them. He sold 20 to 30 properties a year. This strategy for finding leads and small developers could be one that could change your entire business.

Of course this isn't everything you can find and look up at the courthouse. Liens, judgements, divorces, violation etc are filed every day in your county. It takes a little work to figure out how to get this data, but I guarantee if you learn how, you will be the only agent actively going to the courthouse to get these leads.

Go to www.JasonMorrisPrelistingpackage.com and get my free script book36

Tax liens

I could have put this in the chapter with the court house filings but I felt like it was too important

So every year, if you own property, you have to pay property taxes. It sucks but it happens. Every year, the county you live in auctions off a lot of tax liens at a tax sale. These are all the properties where the owner has not paid their property taxes.

If you go bid you don't actually get the property at the tax sale, what you get is the tax lien. Then if the property isn't redeemed (in SC it is 12 months, other states maybe different) and property taxes paid, you as the tax lien holder get a tax deed for the property.

Basically you get the property.

So a lot of these people are not paying for all kinds of reasons. A lot of them actually have equity in the property and maybe they just don't realize what is happening or do not think they can lose the property to unpaid property taxes.

If you go to your local courthouse, you can get a list of these properties that are going to the tax auctions. You can also get a list of the properties that the lien was auctioned off and it has not been redeemed yet.

Then to make it even more interesting, once the property is redeemed, you can get a list of the addresses that never redeemed the property and lost them to the new owners. The great thing is most of these people are investors and have real attachment to the property. They were just going out there and looking to make a return on their money.

These lists of unpaid tax liens are a gold mine for investors and real estate agents. The problem is, most people will not effectively work the list to actually get in touch with these people and try to list or purchase them.

Go to www.JasonMorrisPrelistingpackage.com and get my free script book38

Foreclosure Auctions/lists

Another strategy straight from the court house is foreclosures. I mentioned pre-foreclosures, but really that is when the initial paperwork is filed. That could take a year or more for the person to actually lose their property.

However, sooner or later, the property is going to get auctioned off. In South Carolina, this list of properties being auctioned off comes out about a month before the actual auction.

Once the auction for the property is scheduled, the owner has until the actual date of the auction to work something out with the lien holder, sell the property or pay it off.

Not all the time, but sometimes, if an agent comes and lists the property the lien holder will give them an extension and postpone the auction in hopes to avoid the process and actual cost in legal fees.

You can use this list and actually approach the property owners and look for listings and off market deals.

Go to www.JasonMorrisPrelistingpackage.com and get my free script book

This is not the only oppurtunity that exists with these auctions though. These are a great place to network. Most of the people at these auctions are investors. Most have no real attachment to the property except buying it at a deal where they can re-sell it.

Over the years, some of my biggest repeat clients have come from auctions.

Go to www.JasonMorrisPrelistingpackage.com and get my free script book40

Leads you can find everyday

I know that routine and consistency is the key to the real estate business. I thought I would take this last section and wrap everything up and just tell you what daily lead getting practices you should be doing daily.

You should have a daily schedule and plan to do this every single day that you schedule yourself to work.

1. Go through craigslist everyday! It only takes a few minutes. It will auto sort the FSBOs from the other listings. If they don't have a phone number, email them and just ask for their number. Also get those FRBOs from craigslist too

2. Facebook Marketplace - Spend 10 to 15 minutes going through MarketPlace also. Message them asking for the best number and best time to reach them. A lot of them will get back to you. Most agents are

trying to list those FSBOs through a private message.

3. Driving - Make sure you buy a spiral notebook today! You are driving by abandoned homes and FSBOs every single day and just not doing anything at all.

4. Your Sphere of Influence - you don't have to contact them all everyday. But what if you printed out a list of all your Facebook friends and sent just 3 to 5 messages a day. Just a hello and a message relevant to one of their recent posts.

5. Expired listings - What if you called them each day? Or just just picked an area within 10 minutes of your home or office and just door knocked only the ones that popped up in that area?

Go to www.JasonMorrisPrelistingpackage.com and get my free script book

Bonus 1: The $100,000 notebook plan

I wanted to put an action plan together for you that has been successful for me over and over.

(You can use this for every lead type mentioned in this book!! The same plan!)

This is not a guarantee, this is a plan that will require you to work. Everytime I have gotten in a little slump prospecting or needed to get my business jump started again after taking some time off, this has worked for me.

The numbers I am going to use are from my own personal experience.

Before we get started there are a few things you need:

1. A subscription to an expired service that will give you new plus old expired leads (preferably redx - www.JasonMorrisREDX.com)

Go to www.JasonMorrisPrelistingpackage.com and get my free script book43

2. A dialer will make things a whole lot easier (I recommend the redx Storm Dialer)

For the purpose of easy math we are going to say that every listing you take and sell is worth an average of $5,000 in commission to the listing agent. That is about a $165,000 home with a 3% commission going back to the listing agent.

So for this plan we are needing to add to our "hot lead" notebook 20 leads that we have had meaningful conversations with. I talked about this in the section titled "How your expired listing business will look". You can find lead sheets in the back of this book.

Step 1: Get Leads

Contact Redx about getting every expired and FSBO lead from your market for the last 12 to 18 months. I would not be scared to go back 2 years. A lot of these old leads still want to sell, it just expired and in most cases the market has changed enough that they can possibly get more money for their home.

Go to www.JasonMorrisPrelistingpackage.com and get my free script book

Step 2: Schedule time for Massive Action

This plan isn't for the agents out there that are not committed. This plan is about adding an extraordinary amount of future income to your business, you are going to have to do a lot of work for a short period of time.

Look and see how many leads you have. For this example, I am going to say you got about 2,000 expired/fsbo leads from the last 12 to 24 months. Some markets may vary, some markets you might get more. Call Redx, tell them I sent you and ask their tech support. They are super helpful.

What we are trying to figure out is, how long will it take you to go through all of these leads, calling them.

If you are hand dialing, in the past I have been able to dial 40 numbers an hour. However, that pace is wasting NO time. It is being super focused and dialing like a crazy person.

At 40 dials per hour 2,000 calls would take you about 50 hours.

This is where a dialer really comes in handy. With a

Go to www.JasonMorrisPrelistingpackage.com and get my free script book45

dialer you can comfortably dial about 80 numbers per hour. You are not going to procrastinate over the next call or even have to leave voicemails. You can record 1 message and have it auto drop them for you. The extra expense will save you a significant amount of prospecting time.

At 80 dials per hour, 2,000 calls take about 25 hours.

We are going to assume you have a dialer and you could show up to the office, bringing your lunch and probably get through these 2,000 number in about 3 days.

Step 3. Making the calls and a script

These calls will be tough, you will get a lot of rejection in a short period of time, but you are going to add a ton of future business quickly. Plus these old leads, do not have many agents calling them!

Your initial script will be very simple, here is an example:

Hey Mr/Mrs seller. This is (Your Name) with (realty company). I was calling you about (property address), would you still be interested in selling it?

Go to www.JasonMorrisPrelistingpackage.com and get my free script book46

They will say "yes" or "no". If they say no, thank for their time. If they say "yes" continue with the expired script you will find in the back of this book. If they give you a "Maybe" answer, take it as a yes and continue the script.

What I have found when I do this is that about 1% to 1 ½% of your list will still be interested in selling their house or doing something with a property in the next 30 to 90 days.

If you call this list and then all the ones you didn't get to talk to, you call them a 2nd and 3rd time, you will get an additional ½% to 1% that will want to sell their house in the next 30 to 90 days.

So a list of 2,000 leads on the low end will give you, on the low end, about 20 hot seller leads. Based on my experience calling that 2,000 person list 2 to 3 times during a 1 week period you could fill your notebook with 40 to 50 hot seller leads.

The problem with this plan is, most agents will not do it!

Step 4. Follow up

Go to www.JasonMorrisPrelistingpackage.com and get my free script book

Now that you have sorted through the massive lead list, your job is to follow up with these leads. Afterall, that is our job right?

By following up, you need to have a focused follow up plan where you are touching base with them at least once a week.

****

Following this plan and doing this monthly, even if you just make the calls for 1 day, would potentially be HUGE for your business.

I met an agent about 10 years ago that followed a similar plan and for 1 weekend out of each month, he scheduled 3 days of calls. He told me that he rented a cheap hotel room so that he had no distractions from the office, his family or anything. He would make calls for about 10 hours a day in the hotel room and then go home.

He would take all of the leads he got from those leads and the ones he had from the months before and just follow up with them.

The rest of the month, his work schedule was super easy. He scheduled an hour to two hours a day

Go to www.JasonMorrisPrelistingpackage.com and get my free script book48

(Monday through Friday) for follow up calls and then just went on appointments. He typically carried around 20 to 30 active listings and they were all taken care of by a licensed assistant and a showing service.

This guy had the hours of what most of us would consider being a part-time agent, but he was pretty consistently making about $250,000 a year.

Go to www.JasonMorrisPrelistingpackage.com and get my free script book

Bonus #2 Building a Massive followup Plan

What you need is massive deliberate follow-up

You want to double your business, and you are already making calls, you need to double, triple and 10x your follow up. This is how you are going to increase the number of appointments and the number of FSBOs you are listing. Massive follow up!

In this chapter, I am going to tell you why follow-up makes the difference when getting listings and then I am going to walk you through my process to Design a massive follow-up system for sellers.

One thing I want to go ahead and get out of the way is, I do not automate a drip campaign. I think that is a huge mistake agents make. Everyone is looking for an easy way. There isn't one. There may be some things you can automate like follow up notifications, but a 15 or 20 email canned email sequence is not something that will work in today's market.

Go to www.JasonMorrisPrelistingpackage.com and get my free script book50

Most agents have a "catch you when I can system, meaning they follow up if they don't have anything to do and they happen to see the person's name on their desk."
There is a cool off factor in our business. Most agents don't understand this, but there is a cool off factor in every business.

This is an example of what I am talking about

Let's say a driver see a police officer on the side of the road. How long will that driver slow down?
1. 5 miles
2. 5 minutes
3. Less than a mile

Most of us will slow down for less than a mile. This is the cool off factor. People have very short memories. Most real estate agents are very bad at keeping up with people. With buyers and sellers when you are Out of sight you are out of mind.

I am going to tell you what most agents do, and then I am going to give you an example of what my follow up system looks like.

First I want to give you an example of what most

Go to www.JasonMorrisPrelistingpackage.com and get my free script book

real estate agent follow up systems look like. So you just hung up with a fantastic potential client. You had a great meaningful conversation (by meaningful, I mean they told you all of their deep dark secrets about selling the house down to the penny of what they needed to walk away with and how he just got transferred with work and has to move). Now you are sure you are going to list this house, but this is a crazy week, and he says "call me on Monday."

How many times has that ever happened to you? I bet this sounds very familiar.
Well, today, the day you talked to him is Tuesday. So by Wednesday, he kind of cools off a little bit,(the cool off factor takes effect) he doesn't hear from you, no emails, no text, no pre-listing package. Thursday rolls around, he has talked to a couple more agents from his craigslist ad he threw up the night before. Now it is Friday, Mr. Seller does not remember your name. You haven't followed-up. Out of sight, out of mind.

So come Monday, 6 days later, when you call, he does not know who you are, never heard of you, he doesn't remember talking to you. There is so much clutter and competition out there, a week later (depending on the market) he talked to 10 other

Go to www.JasonMorrisPrelistingpackage.com and get my free script book52

agents already. All of them used scripts and were better and more confident on the phone than you. You had 6 days where you gave an opening and let another agent get involved in the conversation you were having with that seller. By the time you talk to him, it has already been on MLS for 2 days.

So your job once you have a serious conversation with a listing prospect is to do 2 things.

#1 keep them hot on you - stay in front of them - Do not let them go
#2 keep them hot on selling their house

If you've built a good rapport, you do not want to lose that, and you need to keep that conversation going. Hopefully you made a good impression; hopefully you told him you were sending over your pre-listing package, and you actually had one to send over.

Hopefully you followed up by text as soon as you hit send on the pre-listing package.
Do not mail this package initially unless the seller still lives in 1982 where the internet didn't exist. By the time the mail gets there, you have given another agent a chance to step into the

Go to www.JasonMorrisPrelistingpackage.com and get my free script book53

conversation! Mailing this package is the last resort to get it to them.

Now the whole real estate sales process in today's world revolves around trust and respect. I am a big believer we use to broker information. When I first started selling real estate we brokered information, 10 years ago we brokered information, now that information is widely available to the general public. Now we broker trust. Every minute, every day the prospect does not hear from you this trust and respect level you built on that initial call starts to fall off.

Now I want to tell you what my follow-up process would look like with this same seller.
After I talk to a potential seller, I get their email - My favorite line I use is "Hey, Mr. seller, I want to send you over some information about me and my company, that way you know who you are talking to (or you know who is coming by your house). My pre-listing package goes out within an hour. It is all set up on my laptop. I just drag and drop it.

Then type up an email. Now that email is very important, you want it to reference the seller point of pain. The point of pain is the reason they told you they are selling. You want this email to be confident

Go to www.JasonMorrisPrelistingpackage.com and get my free script book54

and strong. Do not write "I think we can sell your house" write "Our marketing works, I know we can sell your house." If you do not have confidence in yourself why should they have confidence in you?

Then I text them as soon as I push send, with just a short text "Hey, this is Jason Morris, I want to make sure you got my email."

The next day, day #2 I'm calling him "hey I wanted to make sure you got my package and see if you have any questions about my company and me?" I answer any questions - I then try to close for an appointment again. I try to close for an appointment on every call.

Day #3 I call and say "I was on MLS this morning looking at homes in and around your neighborhood, is yours a 3br? (Confirm the stuff you guys talked about)". Next I confirm the price. Then, I try to set another appointment. "I know this week has been a little crazy for you, I know you have to get this place sold, so you can _____(whatever reason they told you). I would like to go ahead and meet you this weekend? Would Saturday morning or Sunday afternoon work for you?" I try to set the appointment again.

Go to www.JasonMorrisPrelistingpackage.com and get my free script book55

If they say no, I try to set a time and day for next week. If they say call me back on Monday, put them in your calendar for Monday. But send him over your net sheet - with a short email "hey I worked this net sheet up to give you an idea of what you will walk away with. I will bring all of the information with me when we meet next week."

So in this scenario between your initial call and your follow up call was 6 days.

My first follow was under an hour, my second one was under 24 hours. In the first 24 hours you sent an email, you sent a confirmation text, and you called to follow up. By Friday you have made 4 to 5 contacts. Other agents have made 1 call.

Plus every followed wasn't being pushy or salesman-y, it was offering something of interest to them. I offer help each time. I always follow up with the mindset of helping and educating. As far as most people are concerned, by the time Monday rolls around I am working for them. I tell sellers "I do a lot of work before coming to someone's home."
I have never had anyone say "hey I didn't work with Jason because he just followed up too much, the guy kept me too informed."

Go to www.JasonMorrisPrelistingpackage.com and get my free script book56

Now make sure you use those motivating factors you talked about in the initial conversation.

Now what to do if you call Monday and you don't get them on the phone? Who has a great CRM they are using? If you don't have a CRM, get yourself a spiral notebook to start out with. You need something to keep up with all of your potential clients.

You need some sort of system to keep up with people.

You need to record every action you take. If you work on a CRM, you can automate your follow-up, and by automating, I am not talking about spam follow up. I am talking about it automatically schedules when you need to follow up.

So let's say Monday you can't get the seller on the phone. You need to text and email. "Hey, you wanted me to follow up with you today, just left you a voice mail. Give me a call at your earliest convenience.

Do you see where follow-up makes the difference? if you were that average agent competing for the listing with we, who do you think would get it?

Go to www.JasonMorrisPrelistingpackage.com and get my free script book57

If you can't get in touch with the person when you call, send an email and a text, for the first 10 days. You can go longer, but typically I have talked to most sellers within 10 days.

You need to vary your follow up times you are calling. By my follow up attempt 7 or 8 with no answer my messages are typically, "I have been trying to get in touch with you, do you still want to sell your house?"

I believe most listings will take 12 to 14 follow ups before setting the appointment and taking the listing. You can get lucky and get the listing sooner.

Go to www.JasonMorrisPrelistingpackage.com and get my free script book

Bonus #3 - 10 follow up call, email and text scripts to use for your seller leads

Here is your new follow-up system. Use this as a template and design your own. DO NOT USE CANNED EMAILS FOR SELLER FOLLOW UP , they just go to spam anyway.

You can create templates to save based off of these scripts

Follow up #1

The first follow-up is your pre-listing package. If you guys do not have a pre-listing package, you need to put one together this week. This needs to be your top priority. It does not have to be elaborate. If you want to use my template go to www.JasonMorrisprelistingpackage.com and download it for free.
Go to www.JasonMorrisPrelistingpackage.com and get my free script book59

This one thing is going to change your business

When I don't set an appointment – I hold back the net sheet and paperwork – I use it for future follow up

Follow up #2

You text the seller to make sure they got your email. You need to burn it in your brain that your listing business revolves around your pre-listing package. This is the service you offer to sellers that other agents just don't offer. This is what you do to sell a house. As far as you are concerned, if another agent does not have a pre-listing package – they must just "poke and pray." I had an old broker in charge that use to say agents would "poke and pray" they would poke a sign in the front yard and pray it sells.

I have even told sellers this before when they tell me, they are meeting with multiple agents. "Have they sent you their marketing plan? (Answer: No)
Go to www.JasonMorrisPrelistingpackage.com and get my free script book60

Oh my gosh, I hope they aren't going to just put a sign-out and hope somebody drives by?"

You may notice after a little while you just start getting call backs 100% from you sending out this package. More than likely you are the only agent sending this out.

Follow up #3 (the next day)

Call them and say "Hey, Mr. seller, I wanted to see if you have any questions about the information I sent you over. Answer any questions.

Every call I attempt to close for an appointment if I don't already have one. – I was doing some research – Are you going to be home on Thursday? (You specify the day?) I would like to stop by about 4 pm would that work for you?

You specify the day and time – because if you ask "what time will work for you? No time will ever work" they have to call you back. You give them an

Go to www.JasonMorrisPrelistingpackage.com and get my free script book61

opening for one of the most common objections on the planet.

Why do you want to stop by – I can sell your house I want to meet you and take a look at it. You do want to sell your house right?

(They tell you it isn't a good time – I don't want to work with a realtor whatever – just say ok and move on to the next follow up)

Follow up #4 – Depends on their motivation as to when to follow up

Call – I was looking at homes on the market in your area. I want to send you over what I found. The market is changing (because it is always changing) stuff is always going on or off the market.

Try to close for the appointment.

I email the net sheet over to them with what is on the market. I will often detail out my email to some extent. Basically, I will put my whole pricing strategy into a short email.

(I always follow up the next day after I send this) every follow up is with their interest in mind, not your own.

Next day (I try to close again). Did you get the information that I sent you yesterday? Every time you send information, it gives you a chance to follow up the next day about what you sent.

Follow up 5 (usually a week or so will pass by)

Now by follow-up 5 – they probably know who you are – if they don't, then you really need to work on your presentation and emails, etc.

Follow up 5 is (I was in your neighborhood yesterday) It is more of a (I was thinking about you and your house). I know you want to sell your house because of _____ whatever they told you. I

Go to www.JasonMorrisPrelistingpackage.com and get my free script book

know I can sell your house. Let's meet this week. This call is typically a little more aggressive.

Follow up 6 (usually about a week)

So let's say follow up 5 you just really got shut down and didn't set the appointment.

This is the call you make where you say "Mr. seller, I am going to be in your area on Tuesday or whatever day. I wanted to see if Tuesday afternoon was a good time to meet.

Follow up 7 (holiday weekend)

Usually within a month or so you have some sort of holiday where people are off of work and kids are out of school. Use that holiday. Follow up the Monday before the holiday.

This follow-up will go something like "Hey, Mr. seller This weekend is "flag day, 4th of July or whatever holiday" Holidays are always big weeks for my

Go to www.JasonMorrisPrelistingpackage.com and get my free script book64

follow up. "There will be a lot of people off of work and in town looking at houses. I don't want you to miss a buyer. I can get you in my schedule on Wednesday to get your home on the market, we might get it sold this weekend?"

Follow up #8 (my office done this)

This is why agents don't follow up, by this time, follow up is getting hard! Sometimes you have to get creative to continue making calls.

This calls usually goes something like this

"Since I first talked to you, my office has had (_____ number of) properties go under contract. I really thought one of those would be yours. I know we can sell your house and get the price you are looking for. When are you ready for me to start working for you?"

Now if you are at a small office, you need to use the market statistics. "Since we started talking there

Go to www.JasonMorrisPrelistingpackage.com and get my free script book

has been x number of properties sold and x number that went under contract." Don't just use their neighborhood, use like a 1 or 2-mile radius depending on the density.

Follow up #9 (Your neighbor's house just sold)

This is a great follow up – "I just saw where the house down the street from yours just sold and they got _____ for it. I know you want _____ for yours?" Then tell them why or how their house was greater or worse than the one that sold.

Then ask for the appointment again

Follow up #10 (I wanted to see how things were going)

"Mr. seller I was going through some stuff in my office, and I wanted to see if you have sold your house or had an interested buyer yet?

Go to www.JasonMorrisPrelistingpackage.com and get my free script book66

I first talked to you about 45 days ago. I can help you, if I couldn't get you what you are looking for, I wouldn't keep calling you. When you want me to start working for you?"

By this time they know you. You have had 10 to 12 calls and follow-ups with them. You also have sent text and emails.

That is 10 follow-ups. This is the hard thing in the real estate business. The first call is easy, it's the 5th and 10th, and 15th follow up call that gets tough.

Don't take anything you are told from your follow up calls personal. Trust in the process, the follow-up process works.

Once you hit that 10th follow-up just cycle back through follow-ups 4 through 10 again. Holidays are my favorite times to follow up!

Go to www.JasonMorrisPrelistingpackage.com and get my free script book67

Those steps 4 thru 10 – keeps cycling through those follow-up ideas and plans. You need to plan to follow up 15 to 20 times with a prospect before completely throwing them away or adding them to your long term nurture system.

5 years ago I would have told you that number was less, but I believe today as the market continues to improve, we are going to constantly have new agents jumping in and trying to get involved in the conversations we are having with our clients. That is how you need to think about your follow up, expect to follow up 15 to 20 times.

I know your state definition of what your client is, is different. But look at them as these are my clients and I am calling them because I want to help them, and I am the best person that can help them.

Go to www.JasonMorrisPrelistingpackage.com and get my free script book

Go to www.JasonMorrisPrelistingpackage.com and get my free script book69

www.ingramcontent.com/pod-product-compliance
Lightning Source LLC
Chambersburg PA
CBHW071956210526
45479CB00003B/959